LUCKY

FISH

Aimee Nezhukumatathil

TUPELO PRESS
North Adams, Massachusetts

Lucky Fish.

Library of Congress Cataloging-in-Publication Data

Nezhukumatathil, Aimee.

Lucky fish / Aimee Nezhukumatathil.—1st pbk. ed.
   p. cm.

ISBN-13: 978-1-932195-58-3 (pbk. : alk. paper)
ISBN-10: 1-932195-58-0 (pbk. : alk. paper)
I. Title.
PS3564.E995L83 2011
811'.54--dc22

2010047178

Cover and text designed by Howard Klein.

Cover photograph: "Mermaid Tail" by Ellen Yeast (The Eye.etsy.com). Used with permission of the artist.

First paperback edition, January 2011.

Tupelo Press
P.O. Box 1767, North Adams, Massachusetts 01247
Telephone: (413) 664–9611 / Fax: (413) 664–9711
editor@tupelopress.org / www.tupelopress.org

Tupelo Press is an award-winning independent literary press that publishes fine fiction, non-fiction, and poetry in books that are a joy to hold as well as read. Tupelo Press is a registered 501(c)3 non-profit organization, and we rely on public support to carry out our mission of publishing extraordinary work outside the realm of large commercial publishers. Financial donations are welcome and are tax deductible.

NATIONAL ENDOWMENT FOR THE ARTS Supported in part by an award from the National Endowment for the Arts

For Pascal and Jasper—
who make every thing
and every day
bright as a new penny.

And for Dustin—
who always brings light.

CONTENTS

THREE
Lucky Penny

Let your hook be always cast;
in the pool where you least expect it, a fish.
— Ovid

ONE

A GLOBE IS JUST AN ASTERISK

THE SECRET OF SOIL

The secret of smoke is that it will fill
any space with walls, no matter
how delicate: lung cell, soapy bubble
blown from a bright red ring.

The secret of soil is that it is alive—
a step in the forest means
you are carried on the back
of a thousand bugs. The secret

I give you is on page forty-two
of my old encyclopedia set.
I cut out all the pictures of minerals
and gemstones. I could not take

their beauty, could not swallow
that such stones lived deep inside
the earth. I wanted to tape them
to my hands and wrists, I held

them to my thin brown neck.
I wanted my mouth to fill
with light, a rush of rind
and pepper. I can still taste it

like a dare across a railroad track,
sure with feet-solid step. I'm not
allowed to be alone with scissors.
I will always find a way to dig.

A GLOBE IS JUST AN ASTERISK AND
EVERY HOME SHOULD HAVE AN ASTERISK

Before a globe is pressed into a sphere,
the shape of the paper is an asterisk.

This planet is holding our place in line:
look out for metallic chips of meteor

hurtling through the universe. On my drive
to work, I saw my neighbor's lawn boiling

over with birds. Like the yard was a giant lasagna
and the birds were the perfectly bubbled cheese,

not yet crisped and brown. And I was hungry
to keep driving, driving all the way down

to central Florida, to my parents' house
and into their garage, and up the pull-down stairs

in their attic to find my old globe from 1983.
I used to sit in the living room with Kenny Rogers

playing on Mom's record player. I spun and spun
that globe and traced my fingers along

the nubby Himalayas, the Andes—measured
with the span of my thumb and forefinger

and the bar scale that showed how many miles
per inch. I tried to pinch the widest part

of the Pacific Ocean, the distance between me
and India, me and the Philippines. The space

between the shorelines was too wide. My hand
was always empty when it came to land, to knowing

where is home. I dip my hands in the sea. I net
nothing but seaweed and a single, dizzy smelt.

KANSAS ANIMALIA

I curtsy to the prairie turtle, running with all its might
to catch the paint line of a country road.
I pity the lone ostrich at the Wichita petting zoo,
who plucks out her own feathers because they sold
her mate to a place in Toledo. I cheer the prairie dog, who
keeps watch on the outskirts of his town, knows exactly
where to find a crunchy spider for dessert. Most of all,
I sing for the two-headed calf who managed to live
three whole days before it knelt beside its mama

and sank into the mud. Praise the mud and its confusion
with each quick slip of hoof. Praise the double song
of sadness from the sleep-sloppy mouths. Praise the farmer
who finally sussed it from the sludge and onto his back
while the mama kicked the farmer until he split open.
Praise his daughter who spied it all from her window.
Years later, she'll still have nightmares about that day.
The smell of linen and butter always bring her back.
Praise each groan and sigh from her fretful sleep.

FORTUNE-TELLING PARROT

IDUKKI, INDIA

I will pick
a black card

of luck for you:
star, pinkmoon,

mirror, ostrich eye,
and jasmine bloom.

You may want
to ring my neck

with a tiny strand
of lantana if you don't

like what you see.
Or tear my red beak

in two angry pieces
like a pistachio.

My man covers
my cage at night

with a tattered
turquoise sari.

I sleep with one eye
open, just in case

a white cricket
creeps my way.

LETTER FOUND AT THE TOWER OF SILENCE

(In ancient Mumbai, India, bodies of the dead were placed atop a tower
of silence—exposed to the sun and to birds of prey.)

Dear Feather of Sly Bird Who Nibbles on My Arm—

    Dear Small Wind Inside Cardamom Pod—

        Dear Mushroom Blooming from My Side—

My body drying under the sun is the ultimate act of charity
for birds and mice.

    Sometimes a peacock saunters at the base of the Tower, a shot
of blue to nip me.

        There is no need for melon slice, no need for a bite

        of talk, absolutely no need to write me back—

FOUR AMULETS FOR A FRIGHTENED FARMER

BAGUIO, PHILIPPINES

eel stone

The white square stone found inside an eel's head. Dry it, and roll it
in your hand. Can you hear the tinny music of the bone? Beetles
you have never seen before will wind their legs in protest.

banana stone

On a moonless night, leaves point skyward and you may see
whole devils tripping over themselves just to peel into this fruit.
Watch out for the cleft of their pointy chins.

boa stone

The large snakes have a nail concealed under their tails. Break it off
while the snake is still alive and place it under your tongue. Speak
slippery syllables of a language you once forgot.

fire stone

When someone is burned to death, find a crispy calculus
from that spot. Let the spirit of that crawling stone shake
your pocket. You will be so rich.

CORPSE FLOWER

And when the farmer saw the giant flower

with smell like   bad fish and   bad sugar, he could not look away.
The purple skirt
of the bloom begged him to return.

And so he did—with a pail of water—and sang to it
and caressed it and swiped beetles away
from the blossom's lip.

He even gave it a name and when the farmer
said the name out loud, the flower began to move—
then completely devoured him.

*

Villagers searched and searched for the farmer.
When they too stumbled upon the large blossom,
they decided to name it

after a beautiful jaguar
that once killed several children.
But this flower does not want
to be named.   Does not want   to be owned.

When the flower heard the name,

it stretched to the closest person
and ate her—

ate the name as well.

PAPER PERSON

　　　　I trace paper's origins
to ancient China, where a eunuch
in the Imperial Household collects
wasps. He watches them bounce
against oiled panes of linen, chew
mulberry wood into a pulp and spread
it into thin walls, spit casings for a whole
ochre nest to spin in their sleep.

　　　　How did he first think to copy
these wasps? And what of the hot welts
on the tips of his fingers, and a whole
bracelet of heat around his wrist?
Did the welts interfere with his calligraphy,
each inky curl glowing black on flat silk
and brushed fatter than usual? Crispy bodies
collect near his candle, a light pile of wing
and mandible rolled into striped
commas, and still—he writes.

　　　　I wonder about the space
between his legs, the void of tailed cells,
his skin there so alive with stringy nerve
but hardly touched. No chance for it to grow
resistant to a brush of the tiniest hand,
the coolness of a jade ring. His skin
there thin as the very paper
he first dried and cut clean.

A NATURAL HISTORY OF THE COLOR RED

1.
The search for red pigment was like biting
into a pie that you know is too hot: you do it
anyway, and fast, and with such vigor.

2.
In 1785, Captain Parker ate several of The Fruit, laced
with biting insects, of which he still did eat, and wrote,
"[My] lips were deeply tinged and filled with small prickles."

3.
Each earlobey plate of cacti holds the wee white insect—
the cochineal—chock-a-block with dark staining juice in its belly.

4.
Captain Neilson sailed into Calcutta in 1795 with banners
and boom, announcing he had boxes and boxes
of cochineal (stolen from the Portuguese).
When his men snapped open the boxes for all
the merchants to see, every bug was crisped
into an asterisk, save for three—their waxy filament
and wings busted and bent like wire hangers.

　　　　　　　　But they could still eat.

5.
Munch-munch, munch-munch.
Chibber, chibber, chew.

6.
As curious as a hill sloped with cinnabar—
you were the Apple of My Eye, My Shiny Scarab,
My Deviled Egg. But you've abandoned my ship,

ground my axe, added fuel to my fire.
You cost me an arm and a leg.

You are an elephant of elements.

7.
The insect's only market demand today
is to make our pie fillings look more cherry,
make hunks of ham look more hammy—
and make us look always flushed—
but we blush, even when we are alone.

THE FEATHERED CAPE OF KECHI (A FABLE)

first exhibit: *Anemone*

Kechi sent his son outside to gather feathers of the family parrot. Kechi's
finely feathered cape was now spotted like the fine paperskin of a calf
because of the many bare spots. Each spot glowed a corolla of grease and
candlewood. For the good feathers, the parrot needed only a small start, a
fright, a squawk. The son tamped the soil / the feathers / the seed with
his sandal. Always so many feathers outside because the parrot was a
'fraidy-parrot.

second exhibit: *Scallop*

One day the son came back with only a fistful of feathers. The parrot finally
saw him approach and this time only spilled her tray of seeds and turned
away. Not nearly enough feathers left under the parrot swing to replace what
the father lost in battle. The son shuffled over the cool pink marble tiles in
the foyer to his father and waited for the slap that would surely come.

third exhibit: *Wenteltrap Shell*

Instead, Kechi placed his thumb under his son's sharp chin and lifted it up.
He simply stared and stared at the boy who began to chew his lip. More
stares. More feathers. And the boy chewed and chewed. The feathers grew.
Light water on the walls of an already warm glass. More feathers, and
soon—no chin. The family driver sat at the dining table and said nothing,
only sipped his fruit tea.

fourth exhibit: *Bamboo Worm*

There is the sink and the soap but nothing to scrub. Kechi's son had become
a bird, a slender bird with long brown legs. There is the sink, the violet eye,

the squawk, the fright. Sometimes at night, you hear a crunch on the gravel path in the garden and that—that is Kechi's son who does not want to scare you while he searches milfoil leaves. Listen: he is now in the garden, trying to catch a very slippery blue beetle.

AT HUNDRED ISLANDS NATIONAL PARK,
I COUNT ONLY ONE ISLAND

ALAMINOS, PHILIPPINES

where I can see a quiet shelf of sand
to dock our tiny motorboat
and not disturb the pack
of giant clams slurping
their footy mouths
under the surface.

Where typhoon and the snarl
of a jellyfish arm won't snag
my hair to a nest of seaweed
and bangus bone. Out of all
these tiny green islands, there
is only one where you and I

could not think about going
back to work. Instead we'll think
of market bags heavy with mango-song
in each fold of plastic. We'll think up
cups of cooled freshwater for
our afternoon bath, think of a tiger shell

rubbed shiny from worrying it
with my thumb, and sometimes, when we see
a metal spoon or candlestick wash ashore,
we'll think of our other life, our past life—
a world of meaty stews and snow—*snow!*—
that white weather we'll never speak of again.

KOTTAYAM MORNING

KERALA, INDIA

Chickens disturb the pebbles
just outside my bedroom window

as they skulk and search
for bark crickets. The neighbors

still mourn their youngest son,
caught under an oily car.

Four mornings here and each one
rings out funeral song and honk ::

green parrot and slender goat :: a clay dish
full of ghee. Saris tongue the wind,

trying to taste my grandmother's
cinnamon plants and leafhopper wing.

Or the karimeen fish waiting
to be wrapped and steamed

in a single banana leaf for tonight's meal.
A hundred bats fly inside my chest.

I hear them in my lung cave
while I am still. I want to stay in bed

a bit longer, wait until my grandmother
knocks at the door—her glass bangles

the only clink quieting what's inside me.

IF YOU FIND YOURSELF ON A HOUSEBOAT

KUMARAKOM, INDIA

Pick each word carefully
from a nearby branch.
You don't want to be weighed
down with jibber-jabber
or stone fruit. You'll need
a necklace of green parakeets
and neem butter. Notice I never
said compass. Notice there isn't
a single piece of metal to hold
this craft together. Only coir
and thatch—even the mini-porch
and settee are made entirely
of bamboo. And if you ever
wonder how your boat
has indoor plumbing, a stove,
and icebox—hold the urge
to ask your driver. He will be
too busy steering with a stick
plunged into the backwaters.
One tap of water cane and you
can cross a boulevard of toads.
There is no mystery on water
greater than the absence of rust.
The very lack of it only moves
each reed and shorebird to bend.
The question is a blanket
for your shoulders when you
finally reach the shore.
The question is a rope
so it doesn't float away.

AT THE CENTER FOR RETIRED GREAT APES

WACHULA, FLORIDA

Even though it is closed
to the public every day
of the year except one,

the main attraction is Bubbles.
Here, Michael Jackson's former pet
does not need to remember

how to moonwalk or how to fasten
a seatbelt on a roller-coaster.
Instead, he now gives baby chimps

rides on his back and throws sand
when a favorite culvert is full
of too-loud ape pals. Most

of the others were former pets,
rescued from their elderly owners
who raised them as children—

feeding them canned pie-filling,
beer, and even marshmallows until
they grew too large for their cages.

The ones I loiter over the longest
are Hollywood vets: the chimp nurse
from *Passions*, extras from the remake

of *The Planet of the Apes*, commercial stars,
and circus-escapees. One orangutan
had all his teeth pulled so he couldn't bite

the trainer who forced him to ride
a motorcycle twice a day. Now he spends
his days eating his favorite Jell-O—

strawberry—and can barely even
move. He just sits in the last spot
he was placed, waiting for someone

to lug him to his favorite view
of the bright green lake and the swing ropes—
and not once does he ever complain.

PIE PLATE

for Patrick Rosal

A housewarming gift from my turtle friend—
a guy who has no home himself: carries
all his possessions on his back. Can slip
into the sea or sun himself on the beach

whenever he pleases. He gave me this
red shell—inverted, it's a drum—
the tink-tink-tink of cold ceramic and my spoon
like a calling for dinner, and especially, what comes

after. I love the promise of buttery crust and scoop
of fruit. I love what it smells like: home. Some
believe the turtle carries the whole weight
of the world. I want that turtle to put down

his pack tonight and join me at the table.
I promise him here and now that the next pie
made from this plate will pipe hot steamsongs.
Let the grace of my hands form a crust

so flakey and fine, he'll forget his burden,
his heavy step. He won't remember whether
or not he had seconds. Only the curve
of his spoon, the simple lattice of berries.

THE SOILS I HAVE EATEN

The state soil of New York is named for the place where a man lost his
finger to a rattlesnake. The finger lies quiet in the ground. The snake's
great-great-grandsnakes still chitter through this Honeoye soil. Sometimes
one snake gets the idea he can blink his eye. He concentrates on this single
thought. But a slick frog steps on a maple seed, and the snake forgets what
he was thinking about.

*

Each bend of cypress root drinks a soft fen mud. Each beard dangling from
a branch says, I am a dirty man who had soup for lunch. The state soil of
Florida is Myakka—a fancy way of saying, *Sand, sand, sand,* and if you dig
further still? *Watery sand.*

*

Casa Grande is, of course, Arizona's state soil—salty and robin-red enough
to make the bottom of your pant legs blush. Dustdevils whip against a large
house set against the side of Camelback Mountain. The camel's legs tuck
up around palm tree and stripmall. He longs to eat a salad of thorn and
dates. He longs to eat the leather of a saddle. If you squint, you can see the
tongue clean his eye of gnats at night.

*

Harney sounds like a friend who will help you in a pinch. Silty, loamy, good
enough to feed your family and mine too. In Kansas, we sit around the table
and break bread with Harney soil. Good guy, that Harney.

*

Illinois has dark Drummer soil—mottled loam and gray clay. A little bit of
city grit and soybean. A little light and dark. Street corner and silo.

*

Ohio's Miamian soil is like coffee at a bar: medium roast, hickory, a little
dash of guitar and smoke. Where is the waitress with red stain on her
cheeks, old phone numbers tucked into the ticketbook at her hip? That used
to be me. Where is the torn and pilled-up pool table, the dart board, and
the wall behind it pimpled with holes?

TWO

SWEET TOOTH

TWELVE
TWELVE
TWELVE

a.) When I was twelve, I lived
on the grounds of a mental asylum.

b). My Filipino mother was a psychiatrist,
so that meant we lived
in the doctor's quarters—
one of the three big brick houses
that edged the institute.

c). My younger sister and I practiced Herkies—
our favorite cheerleading jumps—
off the patients' bleachers near the softball field.

d). When I was twelve, I aced
the experiments
with celery and food coloring;
they let me skip a whole grade
and get right to The Dissections.

e). I secretly wished my supply
of grape Bubble Yum would never run out
but I couldn't figure out how to blow bubbles
and snap the lavender gum like Sara could.

f). We sold gift wrap and crystals
for a junior high fund-raiser and my mom still asks
Where are all the crystals I bought?

and
Why don't you display them in your house?

g). When I was twelve, I worried about
the darkening hair on my legs.
My mother bought me my first training bra—
no cup, just little triangle pieces stitched together—
and then a slice of New York–style cheesecake
to bring home.

h). Home.

i). When I was twelve, our house
always smelled of fried lumpia
or ginger.

j). We had zinnias
as wide as my outstretched hand
nodding at us in our garden.

k). My school had to create
a whole new bus stop
just for my sister and me,
and everyone stopped talking and stared
when we stepped onto the bus each morning,
smelling of grape gum and ginger roots.

l). Just who *are* these girls?

INSIDE A DIORAMA

"After being kidnapped in the middle of the night from her bedroom window,
Toronto police found Cecilia Zhang's body two days before her tenth birthday."
—The Toronto Star, 2004

Hundreds of paper cranes
dangle in your school lobby.
All your friends and teachers
fold thin paper, even the boy

who pushed you off the swing
last year. His crane is orange,
the loudest color to call you home.
When I was nine, I made dioramas

too: neat shoebox packages full
of silver painted rocks to represent
Mt. Olympus. There was a mini-Zeus,
complete with a mini-Athena doll

climbing out of his scalp,
a fantastic birth. Other dioramas
showed mighty Stegosaurus
in his natural habitat—happy—

eating weeds plucked from
my yard in Phoenix. A dollop
of clay held a tiny yellow-bell plant,
hopelessly out of place, out of proportion

to the dinosaur—but cheery nonetheless.
I imagine you like the yellow-bell—
ringing sun into a darkened room.
Your heart is smaller than my fist, wild

and thrumming to be found. When
you look inside a diorama, everything
comes to life, even the sand tamped
down with glue shimmers. Every

wispy curtain seems to blow aside,
revealing a spectacular sun.

MOSQUITOES

When my father wanted to point out galaxies
or Andromeda or the Seven Sisters, I'd complain
of the huzz of mosquitoes, or of the yawning
moon-quiet in that slow, summer air. All I wanted

was to go inside into our cooled house and watch TV
or paint my nails. What does a fifteen-year-old girl
know of patience? What did I know of the steady turn
of whole moon valleys cresting into focus?

Standing there in our driveway with him,
I smacked my legs, my arms, and my face
while I waited for him to find whatever pinhole
of light he wanted me to see. At night, when I washed

my face, I'd find bursts of blood and dried bodies
slapped into my skin. Complaints at breakfast about
how I'd never do it again, how I have more homework
now, Dad. How I can't go to school with bites all over

my face anymore, Dad.   Now—I hardly
ever say no. He has plans to go star-gazing
with his grandson and for once, I don't protest.
He has plans. I know one day he won't ask me,

won't be there to show me the rings of Saturn
glowing gold through the eyepiece. He won't be there
to show me how the moons of Jupiter jump
if you catch them on a clear night. I know

one day I will look up into the night sky
searching, searching—I know the mosquitoes
will still have their way with me—
and my father won't hear me complain.

::{ CONCERNING SNAKE HIPS }::

Large snakes have hips.

To the poor frog peeping
over the lily leaf, this
is not acceptable.

There is the drum
of the ribboned muscle.

There is the cricket
with a bum leg.

None matter to those
hips.

Forgive the rot
of leaf under the canoe.

Everywhere, we find
green babies lit up
with blood under their skin.

Reconsider the money mulch,
the pick and lean of each branch.

Nothing stops the snake hip
pounding the bongo sound today

for you, for that little frog
who doesn't even see
what's coming.   I want to pinch

that cheeky mess between my thumb
and forefinger—it puts a pinch

of danger in the way.

It puts
the *ssss* in sashay—

REPTILIAN'S LAMENT

Too cold.
Too tongue.
Too bug-eyed.
Too gill.
Too water.
Too fly.
Too cave.
Too smooth.
Too crawl.
Too fang.
Too spots.
Too claw.
Too stripe.
Too shell.
Too egg.
Too mouth.
Too drone.
Too wet.
Too grub.
Too molt.
Too slime.
Too spawn.
Too nymph.
Too night.

THE MASCOT OF BEAVERCREEK HIGH
BREAKS HER SILENCE

for Ross Gay

There are some suits more difficult to remove:
spades, armor, tweed in the summer, light, cups.
Those nights you thought I was home, dateless, studying
for chemistry, memorizing the dates of epic battles—

I worked myself into a lather of sweat for a field
of angry young men. Sometimes they were so close
I could feel their hot breath in the space between my head
and furry neck. Even the captain of the cheerleaders

never went that far. Every hand that once reached
for me still haunts me at the most unexpected times:
as I place vegetables on the grocery belt, or walking
the glow-wall walkway at the Detroit airport.

Something still pulls me to the ground and it's not
the crowd, the scent of cola and popcorn, the tinge
of engine grease, or a truck revving at Homecoming.
If you slice a jacaranda bloom between two glass slides

and place it on a microscope, the corolla will always fight
for the light. If you once posed for any pictures
with me, still have them scattered somewhere in an attic,
look carefully at the dark netting of my mouth.

If you squint hard, you can see my actual teeth,
clenched into a small scream. I was like that every night.
It was high school, after all. I was always cheering
for something. Still am. Something is always worth

cheering for. There is always some cheer
worth something. Cheer for some worth, always.

HOW TO BE A POET

Breath[1]

Spiders[2]

Boxes[3]

Eyeliner[4]

Thirst[5]

---

1. Even though the mudskipper can breathe through his tail, I wouldn't recommend picking one up with your bare hands. At the very least, use gloves.
2. Of course, some cultures throw onions at a newlywed couple instead.
3. Not every box of Cracker Jack has a prize. In fact, as many as 12 percent of the boxes are distributed to stores across the country prize-less.
4. Eye paint was used in ancient Egypt as a sort of insect repellent throughout the summer months especially. You can imagine insects were much larger then: locust, scarab, giant crickets.
5. Eight glasses of water is recommended, but not required.

SUPPOSE YOU WERE A MORAY EEL

when ancient Romans kept glass aquariums filled to bubbling with your brothers and old Licinius Muraena himself loved to throw slaves in the water, where men were stripped to bits. You cannot help it—it's in your blood. Witches wear dresses made of your skin, sleek and gleaming. Don't you see how they preen whenever they pass a mirror? In the Ozark mountains, I met a man who swears cooked eels turn raw if they are left uneaten and so everyone—even children—eat them quickly. They don't want to feel the slip and bite under bed sheets that night. You move me. You move me *anguillform* and backwards, zipping through the sea with only a quick-stop for shrimp and other creepy crawlies. Your acorn heart sees the future—does it hold a *Valentine, Be Mine!* or a glassy, spectacular car crash? I am mostly blind, like you. Let us wait here in this coral cave and count the number of smelt that swim by. Let them go, all of them. Wait instead for what your thin veins forecast, what they decide to pulse for and where.

BIBLIOMANCY

(the old practice of using books to determine whom you will marry)

Begin with a thick book splayed open
on a kitchen counter and watch the way

the girl stabs and stabs at it with her eyes
closed. The little teeth-bites on the page

mean a screaming—the way peacocks screech
with disgust whenever they catch sight

of their own clawed feet. Each word pokes out
a new promise, a fortune, better than any cookie:

she will meet a boy who keeps smooth rocks
in his pocket. This is how she knows to listen for him.

FRUIT THIEVERY: A LAMENT

AVON PARK, FLORIDA

Wind made my parents nervous wrecks.
Their yard crammed with fruit trees
grown from seeds smuggled in a pocket

or a shoe: lychee, jackfruit, chico, papaya.
Each heavy fruit gently tied with pantyhose
sways in the neck of hurricane. They pray

for the wind to stop so their fruit will be safe.
They don't want to lose now. They waited
three years for a single mango to show, two

for an orange, and one before someone
actually shoveled out their pomegranate tree
in the middle of the night. My mother followed

the footprints to the edge of the yard:
padlock busted, fire ants scattered
into a frantic mess. My mother said,

No moonlight. The thieves must have split
the wormroots blind, pulled the tree
from the sandy soil, while someone else

surely had to run behind—careful to pick up
all the fallen bruised fruit, darkseed secret—
my parents' stormy and still-beating hearts.

LAST SUMMER OF SINGLEDOM

The summer I learned how to make a successful jam, I felt full of secrets.
All the flakes of fish food I tapped into a bowl deliquesced at the surface.
I forgot: no fish. A man said to me, *I am the only exile of Switzerland—you must
love me tonight.* The water on the bar was a maypop vine leading me anywhere
but this smoky scene and initials keyed into the leather of greasy booths.

*

—Where is the bloom?

*

Instead, I flew a thousand miles to Florida and could not begin my tour of
rest without a walk with my mother to check each fruit tree in the back yard:
each seedling, each bud and redburst. Fire ants waited for me to linger too
long while she told of the fruits fallen and given to waste. Or canker. Or
blight. We bent to check the bottom branches for heavy swells about to fall
into the moldy sandscape. *Ixora blossom and strife. Blossom powder and pistil dust.*
The wild and twisty leaves of croton shrubs teething through the gummy
soil. *What a smile, what a smile.* When I returned to New York, to my fiancé—I
only offered him a single gift: two pieces of mango taffy. Of this he did eat
and eat. He kept the wax paper as proof.

THANKSGIVING

The only year I don't remember the turkey
was the year I first dined with the man

I would marry. Blessed be the bowl
of sweet potatoes, mallow melted

in a pool of swirly cream. Blessed be no
seating assignments so I could sit

next to him. Around the table: a physicist,
an engineer, a philosopher, another poet,

a harpist. There were others too, but
I don't remember what weepy thanks

was offered, what linens, or whether
the china was rimmed with a neat print

of ivy or gold. But I've committed the soap
and clean blade of his neck to memory.

I know the folds of his oxford, a bit
wrinkled from a long drive. During dinner,

the physicist said *A cricket won't burn*
if it is thrown into a fire. Everyone laughed.

Some wanted to find a cricket to see
if it was really true. But this man—the man

I married—he grew quiet. Concerned. He's the kind
of guy who would've fished the cricket out of the flame.

SWEET TOOTH

"Violence is as American as Cherry Pie"
—H. Rap Brown

Snakebites are as quizzical as tiramisu.
Your brother is as fiery as baked Alaska.
Peace is as cloudy as rice pudding.
War is as sour as guanabana sherbet.
Fashion faux pas are as passé as canapés.
Suntans are as superfluous as a cream puff.
Revenge is as layered as trifle.
Writing poems is as necessary as a cupcake.
Marriage is as holy as meringue.
A sick infant is as woebegone as a plum tart.
Friendship is as pleasing as buttermilk panna cotta.
Romance is as righteous as leche flan.
Foresight is as benign as beignets.
Wrinkles are as delectable as payasam pudding.
Stockings are as disconsolate as pear cobbler.
Dimples are as wholesome as a chocolate chip cookie.
Park benches are as amiable as pistachio shortbread.
Pride is as wicked as a spice bonbon.
Envelopes are as pensive as apricot compote.
A staircase is as chivalrous as raspberry granita.
Truth is as marvelous as strawberry shortcake.
An elm tree is as gallant as a mint ice cream terrine.
Pumpkins are as convivial as snickerdoodles.
When you hold my hand on a windy day
   while I am wearing my violet coat and tangerine
   scarf, and perhaps a squirrel is raining walnut debris
   from the top of a telephone pole—I am as jubilant as
   butterscotch budino drenched with rum, dusted
   with cocoa powder and topped with whipped crème fraîche.

BAKED GOODS

Flour on the floor makes my sandals
slip and I tumble into your arms.

Too hot to bake this morning but
blueberries begged me to fold them

into moist muffins. Sticks of rhubarb
plotted a whole pie. The windows

are blown open and a thickfruit tang
sneaks through the wire screen

and into the home of the scowly lady
who lives next door. Yesterday, a man

in the city was rescued from his apartment
which was filled with a thousand rats.

Something about being angry because
his pet python refused to eat. He let the bloom

of fur rise, rise over the little gnarly blue rug,
over the coffee table, the kitchen countertops

and pip through each cabinet, snip
at the stumpy paper bags of sugar,

the cylinders of salt. Our kitchen is a riot
of pots, wooden spoons, melted butter.

So be it. Maybe all this baking will quiet
the angry voices next door, if only

for a brief whiff. I want our summers

to always be like this—a kitchen wrecked
with love, a table overflowing with baked goods
warming the already warm air. After all the pots

are stacked, the goodies cooled, and all the counters
wiped clean—let us never be rescued from this mess.

SUPPOSE YOU CHOPPED DOWN
A MULBERRY TREE

Would your tongue cry out in pain? Will it curse itself
for not finding a beveled charm to distract you first?

The white fruit might suffer night sweats. A dry cough.
I know a man who has such a sweet face,
bees follow him down the street. Ants still collect

in the tread of his shoes. As a boy, he once crammed
as many white mulberries as he could fit into his mouth.

His grandparents never stopped him. In college,
he smacked baseballs into a herd of buffalo and when
he jumped the fence to retrieve them, the beasts never

charged or even scattered. I know this man.
I know this dizzy sweetness. I've followed him for years.

If you had cut down that mulberry tree, I never
would have found him. And then where would the magpies
have gathered? What chatty tune would they not sing?

FOOSH

(medical term for "falling on out-stretched hand")

I know exactly what venom and bite to use
to reduce a tall man to tears. The last time
I made a man cry, I hung up the phone
and went out to skate on a pond. The ice

was so clear and thin you could see
the winter-fat carp glide under your boot.
I skated anyway. My handslap must have sounded
like someone threw a block of cheese at a door.

I am a lucky fish. The kind that curls up red
and flimsy in your hand. And the broken center
of it is a spiderweb, threaded through a chico tree
to catch bats. Once, I looked out the front window

and saw my husband in church clothes,
flat on his back. His hand looked like
it was webbed or ready to fly.
Cabbage butterflies can still soar if you pull

off their hind wings, but they cannot pivot
into curlicues like before. The sea snake
has no hands so it's no surprise
it rarely gets hurt. When I hear his name,

I put my hand over my heart when no one
is looking. I want to shield my heart
from that familiar ache, save it, and I do—
with my little sorry and broken bones.

DEAR AMY NEHZOOUKAMMYATOOTILL,

(a found poem, composed entirely of e-mails from various high school students)

If I were to ask you a question about your book
and sum it up into one word it would be, *Why?*
I think I like Walt Whitman better than you. I just don't
get literature, but for a fast hour and a half read, your book

takes the cake. I liked how you organized the lines
in that one poem to represent a growing twisting bonsai tree.
Are you going to get a rude reaction when you meet
that one guy in that one poem? I guess you never know.

You are very young to be a poet. I also like how your poems take
up an entire page (it makes our reading assignment go faster).
In class we spend so much time dissecting your poems
and then deeply analyzing them. I think I like Walt Whitman

better than you, but don't take offense—you are very good too!
You are young. You are young and pure and really just want
to have a good time. Thank you we have taken a debate
and you are a far better poet than Walt Whitman. And I loved

how your poems were easy to read and understand. Hello
my name is Alicia. We read your book and I just loved it.
We also read Walt Whitman's *Leaves of Grass.* There
was no competition there. I liked your book a whole lot better.

It was an easy read. But poetry is not my favorite type
of literature. Sometimes I am offered drinks and guys
try to talk to me but I too just brush it off and keep dancing.
Every once and a while the creepy mean guys try to offer you

things and then they say something. What would you do?
Lastly, I was wondering if you ever wrote a poem that really
didn't have a deeper meaning but everyone still tried
to give it one anyways? Walt Whitman is better than you.

ARE ALL THE BREAK-UPS IN YOUR POEMS REAL?

If by real you mean as real as a shark tooth stuck
in your heel, the wetness of a finished lollipop stick,
the surprise of a thumbtack in your purse—
then *Yes*, every last page is true, every nuance,
bit, and bite. *Wait*. I have made them up—all of them—
and when I say I am married, it means I married
all of them, a whole neighborhood of past loves.
Can you imagine the number of bouquets, how many
slices of cake? Even now, my husbands plan a great meal
for us—one chops up some parsley, one stirs a bubbling pot
on the stove. One changes the baby, and one sleeps
in a fat chair. One flips through the newspaper, another
whistles while he shaves in the shower, and every single
one of them wonders what time I am coming home.

DEAR BETTY BROWN,

"Rather than everyone here having to learn a rather difficult language—do you think that it would behoove you . . . to adopt a name that we could deal with more readily here?"
—U.S. Representative Betty Brown (R–Texas)

If I didn't change my name for my husband,
I'm certainly not going to change it for you.
You can take the time & learn it like
everyone else. I know five-year-olds
who can say it without a stutter or hiccup.
They ring the bell. If I were to change it
to Brown or White or Black or Jones
or Williams or Stevens, I might as well
draw a big fat X across my brown face.
Or if you prefer, I could snip
the American flag into fringy strips
with pinking shears but that would make
the bobbin of the sewing machine that created
the flag unspool whole thready puddles
into the Great Lakes just in time
for the ice boom. & that pop of lake-thaw
into a fragrance of daffodil & lily
would blanket all the neat suburban rows
of ranch house after ranch house.
It would mean jamming my hand into a bucket
of mulberries with my Kansan husband
to signal *summer* & the slow scrape
of leaves across our lawn to signal *fall.*
It means my mother & father each gave
me their names from the coconut shores
of their countries & created a girl
who grew up listening to Elvis while
she did her homework & now writes
poems about people who should know
better & that, Betty Brown—*that* is
as American as a brown betty cooling
on a window sill, as American as apple pie.

THE GHOST-FISH POSTCARDS

First the perfume of cobra wraps around your wrist—then the bloom & bite: summer.

*

I want to dance the itik-itik for you. The tiny steps of duckling & watermoss. Each edge of bread thrown to me will be saved in my little hat & we will share it, share it soon.

*

The islands first appear like cupcakes in the sea, the centers etched out from shrimp & salt. I found you there, singing of sandals & frangipani. Let that be my morning song, my scurry-step, my dew.

*

I had no idea the red fox crept to you in the middle of the night. That explains the lost feathers, the singing of maple seed & so many green spins.

*

Tilapia are little secrets of creation. All pink eggs thread through a filament of light for you to hear. Press your ear to the door. Wait.

*

I loved you dark & late. The crocus have found ways to push up & say this too. The ribbon of my arm's length cannot reach you. & truth be told, should not. You are not the extra rain that floods out worm & bird from the new nests. You are the rain that arrived like a telegraph, too late, too late.

*

Your laughter scared the butterflies into flying like violets, little notes of alphabets & grace. Who invented the alphabet of snakes & worms? Prophets that face each day on their bellies?

*

The frog who wanted to see the sea was mostly disappointed. He preferred wing-dance & jump on soft fen mud. No salt to sear his tender thin skin. Sometimes it is better to stay home, stay put.

*

The fugitive of wasps hides in the swell of summertime. A rotten pear
of a face yells at me from the side of a motel. It begs me to pull over &
I do. I drink this summer night up.

*

Everything about him is a mystery. The way bull moose nudge & scrape velvet
from their antlers & begin to slope around the edges of my yard. There is
nothing a moose could want from me nothing I could ever give
& yet they arrive, faithfully, each spring.

*

I know this desert. Where to find hallowed honey-cactus & sunsets
edged with spirit gum as they slip into the horizon. Please don't follow
the coyote tracks. Listen for my call. My whistle across thorn & dust.

*

I do not like it when sharks spyhop—elevating themselves vertical to see
their surroundings above water. I want them to stay submerged, like my
fondness for fried foods & ginger beer. Your eyeglasses.

*

There are stars that are cola-colored. Your word is the window. The
window is the word. Each night the quail calls, "Wet my lips, wet my lips."

*

My mother heard a woman threatening to hang herself with a bra. These
are the worries she brought home to her two girls, hungry for bedtime
story & her sampaguita soap smell. Now she clutches a rake in my garden.
What new hope does she scrape in those beds?

*

The whole planet howls—a conch blown on the beach, a pair of monkeys
grate papaya rind into each other's hungry mouths, a simple bee in a
jeweled tulip. What is your sound & when & where should I listen?

*

The wishes of sand are simple: to slip soft under a tumbling of shells. A slide
into the happy mouth of an oyster. To get stuck & rub into you like
an angry letter. Or sometimes soft as a kiss.

*

Such tenderness in the air: Virgil once gave his pet fly the most lavish of funerals. Meat feast & barrels of oaky wine. Can you imagine the dirge at such an event? Too easy to call it a huzz or buzz. Another humming in this soft earth.

*

The lake thaw means I return to you. I bloom for you. I point my pistil & blade of leaves to you. Frogs start to shiver in the mudbanks, readying themselves for the dancecrawl across the streamy edges of mud. Can you feel the sunspots already forming on your sweet cheek?

THREE

LUCKY PENNY

HEDGEHOG

The Book of Pregnancy Folklore says if
you accidentally step on a hedgehog
while you are pregnant, you'll give birth

to a baby and a tiny hedgehog. For weeks,
I could not shake this image and I wondered
where it could grow. Your hands were only

the size of a quarter and could the animal
rest in the center? Would you be pulled
onto my chest, clutching your new pet

as they swiped the casing from your eyes?
We have meadowsweet dried
and bunched above each doorway

and I know when we aren't looking,
your tiny hedgehog takes a bite. We lose
a little each day. And later when we leave

for church to pray for the uncle
I just lost, the war that won't end,
each other—I'm certain it will nose

around the kitchen, investigate the patterns
of furniture, ponder the new quiet, the absence
of your cry—eager to know what's afoot.

NOTES FOR THE HEARTBEAT AT MY FEET

". . . my little old dog is a heartbeat at my feet."
—Edith Wharton

My geriatric dachshund, you are a sneeze
in the crook of my elbow—the lick of salt
behind my knees, the quick breaths
against my anklebone. More than that,
you are the lone hollyhock in my garden
of weeds, a failed planet in an arrogant galaxy—
the dip and hold of a wooden roller coaster before
the plunge. You are a red muscle that pulls me along,
quick-stepping when you see someone you love.

For nine months I wore three heartbeats—one
the size of a strawberry. You seemed to hear it first,
before any of us even knew, the way you'd rest
your floppy ear against my belly for hours while I read.
Or sometimes, you'd sniff at my waist, then look up
at me—frantic, expectant—like when you corner
a toad on our walks. Old girl: you are the solid line
on a highway—you've kept me from swerving
into a forest with a broken headlight, a mouthful of twig.

BIRTH GEOGRAPHIC

(an auto-bio poem sequence)

1.
When you give birth, there is no map—no bud and burst of compass
blooming in the corner of the page. How do you know where to visit?

2.
My mother had a Caesarean. I had a Caesarean. My son will not have a
Caesarean. He will glance up at the lights in a dentist's office and think only:
Lights.

3.
Suppose you had a ball at birth. A literal ball—one you could hold in your
arms, bigger than a beach ball: I brought my very own to the hospital. Mine
was rubber, a good weight, blue. A whole planet beneath my legs. Nowhere in
that world was it cloudy. In between contractions, I rocked and rocked on the
Earth and it was good.

4.   [[In the Philippines]]
It is said that if a woman has a lot of blemishes on her face, or if the face
        changes shape, the baby will be a boy.

It is said if the mother glows and radiates beauty, the baby will be a girl.
It is said if a mother is craving sweets and other carbohydrates, the baby will
        be a girl. It is said if a mother is craving oily or fried foods, the baby
        will be a boy.

> *I only craved sleep, so I thought*
> *for sure I would give birth to a pillow.*

It is said the mother cannot eat anything slimy or she will miscarry.

It is said the mother should eat fish (especially bangus) to make her child
        smart.

It is said the mother should not eat mango to avoid having a hairy baby.

Oh, dear heart—
I fear we may have a very smart and terrifically furry child.

5.   [[In India]]

My father was the first of six children born at home, in the kitchen, surrounded by tin bowls and cups, cinnamon, and coriander. It was an easy birth. He was an easy child. This is all I know from my grandmother. I once tried to ask him about it when I was first pregnant: You were born in the kitchen?
—Yes.
His cockatiel squawked in the next room. He brought it to his shoulder. It sat there while my father continued to read the newspaper.

And that is all I know.

6.

When a female bower bird arrives to inspect the male's nest, the male struts and sings. He hopes his carefully decorated entrance and "avenue" will entice her to stay. To this end, he selects all manner of blue decorations to line his nest: pen caps, flower petals, berries, chips of shell, bits of foil. All blue. If the female leaves—he will simply wait, hope for her return, and pass time by constantly fine-tuning the placement of each knick-knack, each twig and snap of branch.

7.

I had   a birthplan—Xeroxed and stapled, slipped   into

a manila folder   for easy distribution   among

the nurses when I arrived at the hospital. I had a doula   who

was supposed to "hold the space" for me.   Everyone slept.

Even the doctors.

Everyone slept   except my valiant husband

who stayed awake   for almost three days

and stayed   strong as a pepper plant.   He was starlight

and samosa and every good thing   I could actually see

him   even though I had my glasses off. My three-page

single-spaced birth plan shrank into one sentence—"Mother alive,

baby alive." And when my husband wasn't looking, I snipped it

to just two words:

8.
Baby alive.

9.
Oh where was the Knight of Knives to rescue this lady in the high tower?
Where was the sword, the halberd, the red banner?

It was my decision. Mine alone.

10.
No one suggested   I get it done. No one even whispered it,

or maybe they did—

but I never heard it. I would have fire-screamed them out

of my sight. After thirty-two hours of labor
and no drugs, my body frame

simply gave out.   I pushed twice and leg-wobble.   More leg-wobble. I looked at my husband   and he nodded *Yes.*

I was a table with no legs,

on a table with no legs, transferred   to another table and bitten

in my back   like the bite of lemons

in your first sweaty drink of the summer: *Delicious.*

11.

My mother promised me her special dessert when I finished, so I focused on
that: alligator pears (avocados), mashed with milk and sugar, a little dollop
of ice cream.

12.

When I couldn't focus on sugar, my husband held my hand in front of the
blue curtain and when I felt the tug—I focused on his sweet face. All the
chrome and shine in the room could not match the brightness of his smile. I
was a fish, a happy fish. I finned up to meet his face. My husband was all the
bright lure I needed until I was caught. When I was caught, I didn't put up a
fight. I lay there and let them do their beautiful job.

13.

Memorial Day weekend: everyone was supposed to be at the beach for a
picnic. They hauled me up for the double chord and catch. And inside me:
a boy who, I promise you, smelled like the sea.

14.

Directions for Assembling a Bluebird Nestbox:

a)   Position one side approximately ¼ inch beneath the slot flush with the
      edge from the back and nail from the back.
b)   Nail the other side, taking care that both sides are even.
c)   Position the bottom centered on the nail holes and nail through each
      side. The top will be higher than the sides. This allows for
      ventilation.

d)   Slip the beveled edge of the roof into the slot and screw it down tightly
using a #8 ¾-inch brass round-head wood screw.

15.
Because I know talk like this frightens you, I will say this only once: If I am
ever lost or someone ever wonders if the cause of my death is by my own
hand—let it be known that I will never leave you on my own accord. Never. If
someone takes me, I will scratch and bite until I gargle soil. My mouth will be
an angry mouth if anyone rips me from you. The center of my hands boiled
with blossoms when we made a family. I would never flee that garden. I swear
to you here and now: If I ever go missing, know that I am trying to come
home.

16.
Oh, *Lord.*
Lord, my bottom lip is bruised from singing Your name.
But it is good, Lord.
We are good.

17.
All weekend long, the dahlias spun themselves into creamy blossoms in the
rain-slicked mulch. What flower should I call you? You arrived too late to
be crocus, too early to curve into morning glory. Here in our tiny town in
Western New York, I was ready to give you anything—a dogwood branch, a
whole solar system, complete with glittery meteors to track. A single orange.
A dark and lucky sharktooth.

18.

Baby, we are *alive.*

UNDER THE PASCAL MOON

(the first Full Moon after Ecclesiastical Vernal Equinox, March 21;
also called the "Egg Moon")

Everything looks like it was washed
with egg. Perhaps there was a crack
in the thaw, hard ground first split
with first shoots of primrose and crocus.

Under this light, the swings empty
themselves of the memory of a small lap.
A robin arranges the nest of mulch
and milktops around her three blue stones.

Five weeks and you still feel the tang
of the knife at your side—the stitch of summer
sewn back into your belly. In the dark—
the baby blinks his eyes at you.

Under this moon, a single car cools its engine,
forgets the cough of commute until morning.
What driveway and roadmarker blown past?
What rest stop and roar will it next learn?

TOY UNIVERSE

In my son's toy universe, all transportation
has a face. There are smiley faces on trains,
race cars, buses. Even his white rescue helicopter
has a jaunty smirk across its windshield.
Plump-plastic cheeks and glossy eyes.
Some frown or look scared with lifted eyebrow
and thinned nostrils. There are stars above China.
There are stars that smell like licorice
and there are stars some children cannot see
because they are piecing together toy trains
and race cars and buses for my child. In the next
universe, let every moon cluster spin each child
a turn on a soda fountain stool and let them pick
out a fizzy creamy drink with their very own
paper straw. Let every comet be a snowball
thrown over a fence to get the attention
of a glossy-locked girl. Let every horse nebula
gallop them into a verdant pasture full
of apple trees heavy with crunchy fruit.

THE LIGHT I COLLECT

*"The baby's foot is not yet aware it is a foot,
and would like to be a butterfly or an apple."*
—Pablo Neruda

If a man in China can keep ten thousand dollars' worth
of caterpillars in a metal box underneath his bed
for medicine, then I want to collect flakes of light
for those winter months when we go a whole week

without seeing a slice of sun. The light I want to collect
is free. Can't be sold as a cure for muscle ache
or to ward off evil eye. I write this in August. It should be
illegal to talk about snow in Western New York now.

I will probably be fined. So many parts
of my newborn son are translucent: eyelids,
his slightly furry nose-tip, the small webbing between
his fingers. When I hold him in the sunshine, even his ears

glow from behind like a church window shining
a celebration within. When he is hungry, I see his feet
kick up from the side of his cradle, motoring the air
like a pumpjack in the Kansas oilfields where his father

grew up. And maybe it's the lack of sleep, but sometimes
my baby's foot feels like a hairless mouse that runs
along the edges of my shirt in search of crumbs
from my last meal. I've been nursing this boy every

two hours in the middle of a record heat wave.
Everyone in town is asleep except for my son and me
and no one even *dreams* of dreams of snow. Without
my glasses, the edge of his foot blurs even more

during those early morning hours until it shimmers

into a perfect peach sold by my favorite fruit farm
on Route 20 where the old lady who shuffles out
to measure my haul of fruit is still in her flowered

nightgown, still in her slippers, and calls me
Sugarbaby, Sugarbaby, Now Where Did I Put My Pen.

LOBISON SONG

I can't hardly believe my geriatric and deaf dachshund
with three-inch-long legs is in any way related to a wolf.
But then she walks in circles on her round, tufted bed
and tamps it down, suddenly she is lupine—flattening

out tall prairie grass for a bed of her own. In Argentina,
the seventh son in a family was assumed to be a *lobison,*
a werewolf. So many furry babies were drowned or left
in a field. In the 1920s, a law said that the country's president

was the automatic godfather of the seventh son, thus
ensuring their protection. My son was born with lanugo—
fine hairs like a furred stem of daisy—across his shoulders
and on the tops of his ears. It vanished after the first

few days, but I can still recall the exact pitch
of his call, roiled from his slick throat. His
was a song of cherries and milky opals—
all gemstone and berry. All fur, quickstep, and howl.

COME HOME, COME HOME

I am the girl in the outfield. I'm the one allergic
to grass. I am the girl in the outfield. I sit
along the third base line and squint for
the pin stripe of your pants, my tiny reflection
in your sunglasses. I know if the ball pops my way,
I will gladly throw my body over our baby.

My clap will be the loudest of all the painted wives.
I am the girl in the outfield. I'll be here through
the night while you practice your pitch. When you
tamp each base bag with your metal cleats, I am
the puff of dust and sand. I am the knock of wing
against each streetlamp. I am the girl in the outfield.

And you are the slam and the run. Or maybe you
are the glove and the bat. You catch all the quiet
between hits or the slide of a shoe across chalk.
I am the girl in the outfield. Our son is the roar
of the absent crowd, and that makes us a triple play.
I am your girl. My hair is a stitch. Come home.

MEMORIAL DAY DERECHO

(a derecho *is a windstorm accompanied by a severe thunderstorm)*

If a bird   frightens a pregnant woman, her   child
will be born   with a wing.   Which explains his feathers,
the claws,   the downy neck. He snipped   my redbreast
every two hours   for weeks, so perhaps   *I* am the bird,
a robin   leaning over his open   mouth,   arranging each stick
of hair for pictures.   But I never   nested. When he was born,
I never bit   into a cloud to sing   a song for the whole forest
to hear.   So maybe   I'm a mealworm   brimming blood. Or
a plastic shard   of a soda ring   tucked into the nest-wall.

*

If I am a bird, then he is a tree. No.   *He is a bird and I am a tree:*

my tumble of hair a dark canopy-crown from the sun,
my heartwood thrummed to bear any weight above
my rooted feet. And perhaps maybe years from now,

as he hikes the Adirondacks and pauses to tie his boot—
maybe he will look up and up—he might remember how he once
reached for me those early days with outstretched arms—
reached for the xylem, the phloem, the dangle of nut-bud and bloom.

ECLIPSE

She's been warned not to sleep with moonlight
on her face or she will be taken from her house.

She wears eel-skin to protect herself. She tilts
her face to the night sky when no one is looking.
During the eclipse, eels bubble in their dark

and secret caves. Toads frenzy in pastures
just outside of town, surrounding the dumb cows

in a wet mess of croak and sizzle. Years later,
she would touch the hand of a green-eyed man
by the weird light. Because of him, she plants

a moon garden: freesia, snowdrops, fothergilla,
bugbane. She is a runner-bean, stretching best

and brilliant in this light. Their child is moon-faced.
She is crazy about them. She is lunatic. She
is taken. She is a hymn book flipped open.

WAITING FOR HIM TO SPEAK

Sometimes she squints, like the queen
whose crown was too heavy for her head.

Sometimes she sighs and the sigh is a pin
of wind through his hair. And his hair

is the tobacco hue of an owl feather.
She repeats colors, her name, his name,

points out cats and birds in his chunky books
and he studies them close, but is silent.

Because of these books, she imagines daily
what it would be like if she were a mama owl

and he were her owlet. Or if she were a cat
and he were her quiet kitty. These are her thoughts

now—not about what color of high-heels she will
wear to the party next week, or the keycode

of a house once given to her by a married man.
She reads her son books about elephants on a bike,

hippos wearing pajamas, and about more owls
who seem to have gotten themselves lost.

There are only about five hundred whooping cranes
left on this planet, three hundred California condors,

and just over six thousand or so beach mice.
During the months that she waits for him to talk,

there will be even less of these animals. She feels guilty
for waiting, for wanting it so badly. By the time

you get to the end of this poem, there will be no more
pygmy rabbits on this earth. The last one will die

as she waits for her son to speak. The nights
are loose, long braids that unravel at the ends. But

he will have his books. He will always have his books.

THE SICK DIET

(based on various food remedies found in Nursing Acute Infectious Fevers, *by George Paul, M.D., 1906)*

Toast Water for when a jaybird flies too close to your son's wee head.

Beef Tea if your skin turns grey from a long day of slide and ski.

Rice Water because you left a good-bye note written on paper made of mummies.

Meat Jelly may soothe your cracked cuticles and will vaporize your dog's wet nose.

Wine Whey clears your eye-whites.

Luap (soda crackers, hot milk, egg, salt, sugar, nutmeg). There is no good reason for this.

Oyster Milk is thought to have a soothing effect on your veined temples.

Milk Punch in your mouth for daemon possession. Taken any time of day.

Junket (milk, sugar, rennet) primarily used for random musings, foreboding utterances.

Farina Gruel sweetens a very sour breath, even if the afflicted is a known gossip, general wrong-doer, hobnobber, or gives acerbic compliments. Be wary of the jaguars and various monkeys that may trail you after ingesting. You can find them slinking down hallways, doors, staircases, and sometimes behind curtains. They cannot be trusted near children nor the geriatric.

TWO EGG, FLORIDA

I want to go back to this town so rich in poultry,
poor in everything else. The women send their kids
to the general store to trade two eggs for a kerchief
full of sugar. Everyone in town gets by with two eggs

worth of sugar—a dentist's dream. They add sugar
to everything: bread, milk, even water, chilled,
for a special summertime treat. Just off the coastline
live pale fish who feast on whale dust. I say *dust,*

because all the fat and wide bones are no more. And imagine
how deep that is—deep enough where the only sign left
of the mighty animal is a vague powder falling onto the back
of a hermit eel who will never see the sun. Beware the jalpari,

the water spirit who drowns young men whenever she wants
company in her watery home. She aches to return to land,
where rockshell and weeds dry out, eventually. Only gifts
of spider lily and sedge left at the edge of the sea placate her.

How lonely would you feel in a place like that—so much pressure,
so much darkness. I'm pulled to the sea floor. My loneliness
is eaten. How poor is the hen that gave one egg at a time?
How do you tell your son to string her neck with twine?

INSIDE THE HAPPINESS FACTORY

THE WORLD OF COCA-COLA, ATLANTA, GEORGIA

Everything about flying in an airplane is a miracle.
The lift of hull and metal. Our collective breath held
in a can. When my red suitcase actually makes it back
to me in Buffalo, I am amazed no one has stolen

the whale shark puppet I've brought home. When you forget
the taste of soil under fingernails, it's time to land.
We make our own happiness. I have been too long without—
this land where my husband farmed and planted rows

of staked tomatoes—a hundred hearts—some split
from too much sun, some still green and growing.
The first time I flew without my son, my chest pulsed
two hot discs of pain whenever I heard a baby cry.

I never told anyone this. We make our own happiness.
I just smiled at the babies, fighting the urge to lift up
my blouse right then and there. And my crooked smile
is now my son's: our bottom teeth do not line up

with our top teeth, but when we smile, we smile big
and bright. We make our own happiness. The final product
comes to us on a conveyer belt. Each light-green bottle full
of fizz-pop and syrup—no machine could ever cap it.

THE LATCH

The days before her first son arrived were spent worrying about The Latch: the perfect hold of a baby's mouth onto a breast, the scoop of lip rolling out a welcome to a river. There were books about The Latch. She read them. There were videos of The Latch. She watched them. The proper way to latch, the painful way to latch. *The Football Hold. The Cradle Hold.* She studied them all, with glasses on. She circled round and round like being pulled in a cart by wee goats on Coney Island. But she couldn't ever get it right. If she thought to wear her silver anklets her Indian grandmother gave her, at least there would be happy bells. Days of cold packs every three hours. Days of tucking torn cabbage leaves into her bra to cool and calm the milk. The bite of a baby is like a prawn claw on your calf. The blade of the unlucky axe that chopped down a jackfruit tree. A cut on your wrist from a broken glass bangle. A sunless forest snake. A mirror cut with a diamond pen. The second time around, with the second son, The Latch becomes a beautiful story. A whole world of skink feet and furred shoulder-blades she could cup with one hand. It will always be summer. There is a plastic pool with little sailboats tracing lazy numbers across the stretch of clouds. Someone is grilling meats. The Latch is the plum and lightning bug. The birdcall and tanned hands. The Latch is a half-closed eyelid and envelope sent across an ocean and the ocean is a bird.

And The Latch is the world.

RAIN: A CATALOG

My son has not yet
found cause to hate

rain. Every plash
into a puddle forms

a plicata pattern
on my dress like

the iris edging
our yard in June.

To make rain
in India, you should

beat the shadow
of the biggest finial

on the Taj Mahal
with your fist.

To this day, janitors
find broken pieces

of bangles scattered
across the courtyard.

LUCKY PENNY

What luck calls to you?
      a) a copper tickle in your palm
      b) the whisper of thread and needle
      c) a whistle

          *

There is talk of getting rid of the penny.
I want to always know the brightness
of a gumball. The Swedish fish sold
between layers of wax paper, a penny each.
Better than blowing on a pair of dice.

          *

One beautiful red cent.

          *

          When is the last time
          you really *looked* at a penny?
              [[[There is liberty in the penny.]]]

Sailors used to chuff a hole in the wood
of their favorite ships to set a penny
for waves calm as Lincoln's sideburns.
          Why keep a penny in your shoe?

And his jaunty collar—did you notice
his throat-nub, the way it hides
mysterious sounds after a meal
of potatoes and a tumbler of milk?

          His bright building on the back—
          can you spot all the people on the steps?
          Witness: the little girl and her balloon,
          the stray dog, nosing around

for clumpy pieces of popcorn. I want to sit
under a tree on the right side of the penny.
I'll bring my sons, who will surely
also want balloons.

And maybe—if the penny ever gets an update—

you'll see a mother who runs
after her sons, the sons who run after their balloons,

the balloons already floating towards the top
of Lincoln's giant marble head.

ACKNOWLEDGMENTS

*

Warmest thanks to the hardworking editors of these fine publications in which this work first appeared, sometimes in different versions:

32 Poems	"Two Egg, Florida"
Asian-American Literary Review	"Dear Betty Brown," "How to Be a Poet," and "Letter Found at the Tower of Silence"
American Poetry Review	"The Ghost Fish Postcards"
Black Warrior Review	"::{ Concerning Snake Hips }::," "Lucky Penny," and "Twelve / Twelve / Twelve"
Blue Earth Review	"Notes for the Heartbeat at My Feet"
Brevity: A Journal of Concise Literary Non-fiction	"The Soils I Have Eaten"
The Concher	"Reptilian Lament"
Connotations Press	"Lobison Song," "Mosquitoes," and "Pie Plate"
Crab Creek Review	"Thanksgiving"
Crab Orchard Review	"Diorama"
FIELD	"Last Summer of Singledom"
Indiana Review	"Baked Goods," "Four Amulets for a Frightened Farmer," and "Hedgehog"
The Literary Review	"Bibliomancy" and "A Globe Is Just an Asterisk and Every Home Should Have an Asterisk"
Lo-Ball	"Rain: A Catalogue"
MiPoesias	"Come Home, Come Home" and "Dear Amy Nehzookoookammyyatootill"
Narrative Magazine	"Corpse Flower," "Fortune-Telling Parrot," "Kansas Animalia," "A Natural History of the Color Red," and "Suppose You Chopped Down a Mulberry Tree"
The Normal School	"The Sick Diet"
Orion	"Kottayam Morning" and "Suppose You Were a Moray Eel"
Pirene's Fountain	"The Latch" and "The Light I Collect"
Ploughshares	"Eclipse"
Poetry International	"Are All the Break-Ups in Your Poems Real?"
Prairie Schooner	"Inside the Happiness Factory" and "Memorial Day Derecho"

The Rumpus	"Paper Person"
Sou'wester	"At the Center for Retired Great Apes"
Subtropics	"The Secret of Soil"
Sweet	"Fruit Thievery: A Lament"
The Warbler	"At Hundred Islands National Park, I Count Only One Island"
Washington Square	"FOOSH," "If You Find Yourself on a Houseboat," and "Waiting for Him to Speak"
Water~Stone	"Birth Geographic"

*

Special thanks to the editors who selected poems from this collection for *The Literary Review*'s Angoff Award and *Prairie Schooner*'s Glenna Luschei Prize.

"The Feathered Cape of Kechi" series first appeared as a featured chapbook in *Black Warrior Review*.

"The Mascot of Beavercreek High Breaks Her Silence" appears in the 2010 *Alhambra Poetry Calendar*, edited by Shafiq Naz (Alhambra Press, 2009), and *Indivisible: An Anthology of Contemporary South Asian American Poetry*, edited by Neelanjana Banerjee, Summi Kaipa, and Pireeni Sundaralingam (University of Arkansas Press, 2010).

"How to Be a Poet," "Bibliomancy," "Under the Pascal Moon," and "Letter Found at the Tower of Silence" appear in the *HarperCollins Book of Modern English Poetry by Indians*, edited by Sudeep Sen (HarperCollins India, 2011).

"Dear Betty Brown," appears as a video in Rabbit Light Movies (rabbitlightmovies.com).

*

I'm so grateful for my esteemed and dear colleagues and students at State University of New York–Fredonia; the National Endowment for the Arts; The MacDowell Arts Colony for taking care of me when I was pregnant and again as a new mama; the Radcliffe Institute for Advanced Study; Anthony Gil, curator of Arizona State University's Natural History collections; The Virginia Piper Writers' Center; and the staff of the Georgia Aquarium and the Monterey Aquarium for answering a million questions during my visits. Thank you to David Citino—always—and Jeffrey Levine, Jim Schley and the fine folks at Tupelo Press, the Parsons Family, JoAnn DeRosa, Sara Sutherland, Sharon Wong, Ron Degenfelder, Americ McCullagh, Bob Hicok, Terrance Hayes, Dorianne Laux, Pattiann Rogers, Joseph Legaspi, Sarah Gambito, Pat Rosal, Jennifer Chang, Oliver De la Paz, Ron Villanueva, Vikas Menon, Erika Meitner, Mary Biddinger, Paul Guest, Joy Katz, Julianna Baggott, Kelli Russell Agodon, Beth Ann Fennelly, Jay Baron Nicorvo, and Ross Gay. Hugs to Maggie Heavern, Rebecca White, Sara Shinder, Leah Urtel, and Susan Kornacki for helping out with my sons in those early months. For Dustin, selfless and true: every day is a kind of Thanksgiving with you. And always: so much gratitude to my parents, Mathew and Paz, for their laughter, their stories, their love.

Other books from Tupelo Press

This Lamentable City, Polina Barskova,
      edited and introduced by Ilya Kaminsky

This Nest, Swift Passerine, Dan Beachy-Quick

Cloisters, Kristin Bock

Stone Lyre: Poems of René Char,
      translated by Nancy Naomi Carlson

Poor-Mouth Jubilee, Michael Chitwood

staring at the animal, John Cross

Psalm, Carol Ann Davis

Orpheus on the Red Line, Theodore Deppe

The Flight Cage, Rebecca Dunham

Then, Something, Patricia Fargnoli

Calendars, Annie Finch

Other Fugitives & Other Strangers, Rigoberto González

Keep This Forever, Mark Halliday

Inflorescence, Sarah Hannah

The Us, Joan Houlihan

Red Summer, Amaud Jamaul Johnson

Dancing in Odessa, Ilya Kaminsky

Ardor, Karen An-hwei Lee

Dismal Rock, Davis McCombs

Biogeography, Sandra Meek

Flinch of Song, Jennifer Militello

At the Drive-In Volcano, Aimee Nezhukumatathil

The Beginning of the Fields, Angela Shaw

Selected Poems, 1970–2005, Floyd Skloot

The Forest of Sure Things, Megan Snyder-Camp

Human Nature, Gary Soto

Embryos & Idiots, Larissa Szporluk

the lake has no saint, Stacey Waite

Archicembalo, G.C. Waldrep

Dogged Hearts, Ellen Doré Watson

Narcissus, Cecilia Woloch

Monkey Lightning, Martha Zweig

See our complete backlist at www.tupelopress.org